'91

THE DAYS
OF THE WEEK

Text © copyright 1989 by Garrett Educational Corporation
First published in the United States in 1989 by
Garrett Educational Corporation, 130 East 13th Street,
Ada, OK 74820
First published by Young Library Ltd., Brighton, England
© Copyright 1982 Young Library Ltd.

Manufactured in the United States of America

Library of Congress Cataloging Publication Data

Hughes, Paul.
  The days of the week: stories, songs, traditions, festivals,
and surprising facts about the days of the week all over the world /
Paul Hughes.
     p. cm.
  Bibliography: p.
  Includes index.
  Summary: Presents a variety of facts, stories, songs, festivals,
and traditions about the days of the week from all over the world.
  1. Days—Folklore—Juvenile literature.   2. Calendar—Folklore—
Juvenile literature.   [1. Days—Folklore.   2. Calendar—Folklore.]
I. Title.
GR930.H84   1989
398.27—dc20   89-11758
   ISBN 0-944483-32-1   CIP
                                                     AC

THE DAYS OF THE WEEK

Have you ever wondered why a week has seven days, or how those days got their names? Have you heard people talk about blue Monday, or unlucky Friday, or Sunday's child? Do you know what the Greeks, Chinese, and Hindus call their days of the week, and what the names mean; and why so many countries have their sabbath on Friday or Saturday instead of Sunday? You can find out all these things here, as well as learn lots of rhymes and sayings about the week, and work out which day of the week New Year's Day will fall, or when your birthday will fall on any year in the future.

People can have different ideas about customs, rhymes, and sayings handed down by word of mouth or translated from other languages. Also, people do not always agree about facts in legend and history. Therefore, you should expect to hear slightly different accounts of these things from time to time.

THE DAYS

Written by PAUL HUGHES

OF THE WEEK

Illustrated by JEFFREY BURN

 GARRETT EDUCATIONAL CORPORATION

Contents

Why does a week have seven days?

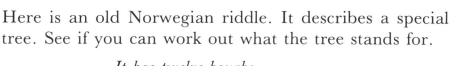

Here is an old Norwegian riddle. It describes a special tree. See if you can work out what the tree stands for.

> *It has twelve boughs,*
> *Four nests on each bough,*
> *Seven eggs in each nest,*
> *   and the seventh egg is of gold.*

The tree is the year. The twelve boughs are the months. The four nests are the four weeks in each month. The seven eggs are the seven days in each week, and the golden one is Sunday.

Everyone knows that a week has seven days — Sunday, Monday, Tuesday, Wednesday, Thursday, Friday, and Saturday. But have you ever wondered *why* there are seven, not four or nine or some other number? It has not always been seven; and in very early times there were no weeks at all.

What exactly *is* a week?

Years, Months, and Days

Years, months, and days are easy to understand. They measure the time taken for the movements of the earth and the moon.

A year is the time taken by the earth to make one orbit of the sun. A year takes us through the seasons of spring, summer, autumn, winter, and back to spring again.

A month is about the time taken by the moon to make

one orbit of the earth. We can watch the new moon (a crescent shape) grow fuller each night until it is a complete circle, then grow smaller each night as it loses a part of the circle until it is a crescent again, one month later. The word "month" is based upon the word "moon."

A day is the time taken for the earth to rotate once on its own axis. The side which faces the sun is in daylight; it gradually spins away until it faces the darkness away from the sun, then continues spinning until it is back facing the sun again, and a new day begins.

These are natural divisions of time. They would occur even if there were no one on earth to measure them. However, weeks are quite different — they were invented by our ancestors.

People of long ago

We got the idea for seven days, and the names for those days, from people who lived thousands of years ago. They were the Babylonians who lived 6,000 years ago; the Jews who lived 3,500 years ago; the Romans of 2,000 years ago; and the Saxons of 1,500 years ago.

Ancient people like the Babylonians found that they needed another division of time, longer than a day but shorter than a month. There were several reasons why this was necessary, and one of them was their habit of holding markets several times each month. They wanted

9

a convenient measure of the time between markets. People of West Africa held a market once every four days, so their week was four days long. The Assyrians (who lived even earlier than the Babylonians) grouped the days into sixes and had six-day weeks. The Egyptians, who lived at the same time as the Babylonians, had a week ten days long. The Roman week lasted eight days.

The Babylonians thought that seven was a very important number. Seven days was about the time it took for the moon to go through each of its four phases — from new moon to half moon, half moon to full moon, full moon to half moon, and half moon back to new moon again. They also saw what they thought were seven planets in the sky — the sun and moon (which we now no longer call planets), Mercury, Mars, Jupiter, Venus, and Saturn. (The planets Uranus, Neptune, and Pluto were too far away for them to see, as they had no telescopes.) Because seven was such an important number to the Babylonians, they grouped their days into sevens and had a seven-day week. They believed that each day of the week was "ruled" by one of the planets.

The Old Testament of the Bible, which was written by the Jews, mentions the number seven lots of times. It says that God created the world in six days and rested on the seventh day. So the Jews, and other tribes who believed in the Old Testament, also decided to have a week of seven days.

The names reach Europe

The ideas of the Babylonians and the Jews spread across Asia, Africa, and Europe. The seven-day week spread, too. In the fourth century the Romans stopped using their eight-day week and adopted the seven-day week. They used it throughout their empire, which covered most of

Europe. They did not use the Babylonian or Jewish names, of course. They preferred to name the days after their own names for the planets. Some of the planets' names were also the names of their gods — Mercury, Mars, Jupiter, Venus, and Saturn. Many of the countries the Romans conquered adopted the Roman language and the Roman names for the days.

After the Roman empire fell about 1,500 years ago, the Saxons colonized parts of northern Europe. They kept some of the Roman names, but named the other days after their own gods.

The seven-day week is now used by most countries of the world. There are no Babylonian, Jewish, Roman, or Saxon empires today, and people of different countries speak many different languages. However, their names for the days of the week are often similar. That is because so many European languages take their names for the days from the languages of the ancient Romans and Saxons.

Many other countries (for example, Australia, Brazil, Canada, India, United States, Mexico, West Indies, New Zealand, and Argentina) speak European languages, and thus the same names have spread over most of the world.

However, other countries have entirely different names for their days, as you will see.

11

Rhymes about the days

What day of the week were you born on? This little rhyme tells you what sort of person you will become.

> *Monday's child is fair of face,*
> *Tuesday's child is full of grace,*
> *Wednesday's child is full of woe,*
> *Thursday's child has far to go;*
> *Friday's child is loving and giving,*
> *Saturday's child works hard for a living;*
> *But the child that is born on the Sabbath day*
> *Is blithe and bonny, good and gay.*

If you don't know which day of the week you were born on, you can find out by looking at the Perpetual Calendar on pages 50 to 57.

Would you believe that even the day you sneeze on can be significant? It's true if this rhyme is to be believed:

> *If you sneeze on Monday, you sneeze for danger;*
> *Sneeze on Tuesday, kiss a stranger;*
> *Sneeze on Wednesday, sneeze for a letter;*
> *Sneeze on Thursday, something better;*
> *Sneeze on Friday, sneeze for sorrow;*
> *Sneeze on Saturday, see your sweetheart tomorrow;*
> *Sneeze on Sunday, the Devil will have you the rest of*
> *   the week.*

Lastly, there is the sad story of Solomon Grundy. Every day of the week seemed to bring another dramatic event in his life:

Solomon Grundy,
Born on Monday,
Christened on Tuesday,
Married on Wednesday,
Took ill on Thursday,
Worse on Friday,
Died on Saturday,
Buried on Sunday;
That is the end
of Solomon Grundy.

Sunday

The Sun's Day

Many early people worshipped the sun. Later civilizations worshipped gods which represented the power of the sun. It was natural that they should name the first day of the week after the sun. The Babylonians believed that the first hour of this day was ruled by the sun.

In the ancient Greek and Roman civilizations the first day of the week was called the Sun's Day. Some of the countries that were part of the Roman empire still call the day after the sun. All English-speaking countries do. The Saxon's way of spelling it was Sonnendaeg. The names that Germans, Dutch, Swedes, and Danes use today are very similar (see chart on pages 46 and 47).

Not only European countries named the first day of the week after the sun. Across the other side of the world, in India and Pakistan, it is also called the Sun's Day.

Easter Sunday

Christians think Sunday is a holy day because it was the day that Jesus was raised from the dead after his crucifixion. This miracle is remembered each year at Easter, and Easter Sunday is the greatest of all Christian feast days. Easter Sunday, which is called God's Day in some parts of America, and Great or Holy Sunday by members of the Orthodox churches, does not have a fixed date, but it always falls between March 22nd and April 25th.

In many Christian countries, eggs are given on Easter

14

Sunday as a symbol of the rebirth of Christ. Every child enjoys coloring eggs and then taking part in an egg hunt at Easter. In parts of America and England people go egg-rolling. Eggs are rolled downhill, and the one that travels farthest or fastest without breaking is the winner. The White House lawn in Washington, D.C., is the scene of the most famous egg-rolling in America. In Australia children make little egg nests out of moss or twigs, which their parents then fill with egg-shaped sweets and hide in the garden for the children to find. In Russia, rich people used to make beautiful eggs of precious metals studded with jewels and give them as gifts at Easter.

The giving of eggs is a very ancient custom. It probably began when Christians gave up eating meat, fats, and eggs for the forty days before Easter. This period of fasting is called Lent. When Lent is over and Easter arrives, it is a time for rejoicing, and eating nice things like eggs again.

Lent ends with Palm Sunday, which is sometimes called Hosanna Sunday. Palm or Hosanna Sunday commemorates Jesus's triumphant entry into Jerusalem, when people spread palm leaves in his path.

Mother's Day

In Canada, Australia, America, and New Zealand, Mother's Day is held on the second Sunday in May. Mother's Day is traditionally a day of rest for mothers. On the fourth Sunday in Lent, usually around the end of March, people in England celebrate Mothering Sunday, or Mother's Day. In Britain it used to be the custom for children to bake fruit cakes to give to their mothers on Mothering Sunday, with a bouquet of flowers or some little gift. The fruit cakes were not to be eaten until Easter. The custom died out in Britain, however, and Mother's Day was forgotten.

Then in 1906 an American, Mrs. Anna Jarvis of Philadelphia, had the same idea of keeping one day special for mothers. The second Sunday in May was chosen to be Mother's Day. The idea spread all over America. In some schools festivities are held on the Friday before Mother's Day.

During the Second World War, American servicemen were stationed in England. They passed the custom of Mother's Day back to the British, who revived Mothering Sunday in its original time in March.

The Lord's Day

The Old Testament of the Bible says that on one day of the week people should not work, but should rest. In the New Testament it says that the day of rest should be Sunday, which it calls the Lord's Day. So in most Christian countries Sunday is a day of rest, when shops, offices, and factories are closed.

The custom of Sunday closing goes back to Roman times. About 300 years after the death of Christ, the Romans became Christians. Their emperor Constantine ruled that throughout all the empire Sunday should be a

17

SUNNE-DEI

SONDAYE

SUNDAIES

SUNDAY

day of rest. He said that all work should cease on this day, except that farmers could work if necessary. The name of the day was changed from the Sun's Day to *dies dominica,* which means the Lord's Day. Some countries of Europe still call it the Lord's Day. In French it is spelled Dimanche; in Italian, Domenica; and in Spanish and Portuguese, Domingo.

For non-Christians, however, Sunday is just the first day of the week. Jews and Arabs call it Day One or the First Day. For the Jews and the Japanese it is the biggest shopping day.

Even in the English language the spelling of the day has changed many times. If there really was a man called Robin Hood living in Sherwood Forest 800 years ago, he would probably have called the day by one of its old English names — Sunne-dei or Sonedae. Henry VIII, King of England from 1509 to 1547, might have called it Sonday, Sondaye, or even Sounday. By the time the Pilgrim Fathers built their first settlement in Massachusetts in 1620, the name of the day would have been Sundaies. When Captain Cook was making his voyages of discovery into the South Seas about 170 years later, the name had become the one that we know today.

Sunday sayings

The word Sunday crops up in lots of expressions, phrases, and sayings. In many different Christian countries around the world people talk of wearing their Sunday best, or Sunday-go-to-meeting clothes, meaning their very best clothes. This expression comes from the time when people could afford to buy only one good suit of clothes, and these were worn only once a week — to church on Sunday.

18

Sunday was also the day when people ate better than they did during the rest of the week. Polish people have this saying to remind them that — though they may eat well on Sunday — they must fast on Friday:

There is a Sunday in the week, but there is also a Friday.

At one time it was illegal for fishermen in Pennsylvania to work on Friday. So Friday came to be called "Fishermen's Sunday," since it had become their day of rest. In Britain, Sunday was pay day for servants. Scottish servants who looked forward to being paid and getting the day off used to say this:

Come day, go day, God send Sunday.

There is also an expression for things that will never happen at all:

Not in a month of Sundays.

In Mexico people say *Domingo siete!* or "Sunday the seventh!" which means "What a blunder!" Perhaps some important person in history made a huge mistake on a Sunday the seventh which has never been quite forgotten.

19

Monday

The Moon's Day

The second day of the week has been thought of as the moon's day from earliest times. The moon, like the sun, was worshipped. Primitive people used to hold festivals to the new moon each month. The moon god or goddess was usually believed to be evil, and it has always been thought unlucky to sleep in moonlight. The light of the full moon was supposed to drive people mad, and the word "lunatic" comes from the ancient Latin word *lunae,* which means moon. The Babylonians thought the first hour of this day was ruled by the moon.

The Romans called the day *lunae dies,* which means the "moon's day." The Saxons called it the moon's day, too. In the language that English people spoke during the Middle Ages it was called Munendai or Moneday. This later became Monunday. The name finally became the one we now know around the time that Sir Francis Drake defeated the Spanish Armada in 1588.

In German, Welsh, French, Italian, Spanish, Danish, Swedish, Dutch, Urdu, and Hindi the day is named after the moon. The Hindi name for the day is Somavara. Soma, the god of the moon, married twenty-seven of the daughters of Daksha, but angered Daksha by neglecting all but one of them. Daksha then condemned the moon god to wax and wane each month. And, of course, that is what the moon does.

The Quakers, a Christian religious sect, believe that God's days should not be given pagan names, so they call

20

the days by numbers. Monday is Day Two. Monday is also called Day Two, or the Second Day, by Christians in Greece and Portugal and by Jews and Arabs in Israel and Arabian countries.

Sad and solemn days

Monday is the first day of the working week in many countries around the world, and lots of proverbs about Monday tell how people feel on that day. In Brazil, for example, there is a saying that goes:

No Saturday without sunshine, Sunday without Mass,
or Monday without laziness.

People who are miserable about going back to work say that they have "that Monday morning feeling" or "the Monday morning blues." In America the day is often called Blue Monday.

For Jewish people, Monday is an important religious day. On Monday and Thursday Jewish synagogues hold special services where worshippers beg God to forgive them for their sins. Very orthodox Jews fast on the Monday, Thursday, and following Monday after the feasts of Passover and Sukkot (Jewish festivals held in spring and in autumn). These three days are called Behab. Very orthodox Jews also fast on Monday and Thursday *every* week.

Happy Mondays

In Christian countries, certain Mondays in the year used to be very jolly days indeed. Until about a hundred years ago the first Monday of the year was a day for giving presents. It was called Handsel Monday, and the gifts were given to children and servants to bring them good luck in the coming year.

The first Monday after the twelfth day of Christmas was called Plow Monday. It was so called because it marked the end of the Christian holidays when men returned to their plowing or other daily work. It was the custom for farm hands to draw a plow from door to door and beg for "plow money," which they later spent enjoying themselves!

The Monday before the Christian festival of Lent was called Collop Monday or Fat Monday (a collop is a roll of flesh on the body). It was a day when people ate eggs, fats, and meat, foods that were banned during the forty-day fast period of Lent.

The second Monday after Easter is called Hock Monday. Until about 400 years ago there was a strange custom in English villages on this day. Women would seize the men, tie them up, and demand a small payment for their release. On the following day, called Hock Tuesday, the men could do the same thing to the women. The money was given to the parish church.

Lucky and unlucky

There are lots of superstitions about Monday. Some people in America believe that couples married on a Monday will have a busy and exciting life together. It is, however, believed to be a bad day on which to have your hair cut. In Europe, it is thought that thunder on Monday foretells the death of a woman. Monday, together with Tuesday, is a good day on which to cut your fingernails!

Three Mondays of the year are believed to be especially unlucky, and all three are connected with stories from the Bible. The first Monday in April is unlucky because it is supposed to be the day that Cain murdered his brother Abel. The second Monday in August was the day when the wicked towns of Sodom and Gomorrah were destroyed. The last Monday in December is believed to be the birthday of Judas Iscariot, the man who betrayed Jesus.

Tuesday

Mars's Day

The Babylonians believed that the first hour of this day was ruled by the planet Mars. The Romans had the same idea, and they called the day *dies martis*, which means Mars's Day. People in many countries of Europe still call the day after Mars. In French it is Mardi; in Spanish, Martes; and in Italian, Martedi. In India, the Hindus also named the day after Mars. They call it Mangalavara. In Urdu, the language of Pakistan, it is called Mangalvar.

The Romans had lots of gods and goddesses. Each one of these was in charge of one aspect of human life. Bacchus, for example, was the god of wine, and Diana was the goddess of hunting. Some of their gods bore the same name as a planet. Mars was the god of war, and Romans always called upon him for help when they went into battle.

Tiw's Day

When the Roman empire covered most of Europe, including Britain, everyone used the Roman names for the days. But when the Romans left and the Saxons settled in Britain, they changed the names of the days to fit their own gods and goddesses. The Saxons believed in the Norse gods of Scandinavia. The king of the gods was Woden, who lived in a sort of heaven called Asgard. He had a great hall called Valhalla where all the dead heroes went. The Saxon god of war, courage, and the sword was Tiw. They named the third day of the week after their god of war in the same way that the Romans did, calling it Tiwesdaeg.

Tiw was Woden's son. He helped Woden choose the heroes who would go to Valhalla. He was a wise and great warrior and was always fighting great battles. In the Norse legends, Tiw fought the fierce wolf Fenris. He managed to bind the evil creature but had his hand bitten off in the fight.

It took about a thousand years for the spelling of Tuesday to change from the Saxon one to the one we know today. In medieval times it was called Tisdei or Tysday. Henry VIII might have called it Tewisday; but by the end of the seventeenth century the name Tuesday had arrived.

Tuesday festivals

For Christian people the most important Tuesday of the year is Shrove Tuesday. Shrove Tuesday is the very last day before Lent begins. In days gone by, Christians confessed their sins on Shrove Tuesday and were forgiven (or, in Old English, "shriven"). Later it became a time

of great festivity in preparation for Lent. The feasting began the evening before when boys walked the streets singing:

Shrovetide is nigh at hand,
And I be come a shroving;
Pray, dame, something,
An apple or a dumpling.

It was a time when eggs, fats, and other foods forbidden in Lent were eaten for the last time. Nowadays in Britain and in parts of America these foods are made into pancakes. Pancake races are held on Shrove Tuesday when people have to toss a pancake in the pan while running.

In the city of New Orleans, Louisiana, Shrove Tuesday is better known by a different name: Mardi Gras. Mardi Gras is French for Fat Tuesday. The fun begins in early January, and people flock to the city to enjoy the costume balls, parades, and joyful celebrations. In Brazil the people of Rio de Janeiro celebrate Carnival. The word carnival came from the Latin *carne vale*, which means ''meat farewell.'' Carnival is a massive parade of glittering costumes, gay music, color, song, and dance in which almost every person in Rio becomes involved.

Tuesday is not always a happy day, however. On the other side of the world, in India, Tuesday is thought to be a very unlucky day on which to be born. According to an old Arab proverb, you should

Never start, never arrive, on a Friday or a Tuesday.

In Europe there is a superstition that it is unlucky to meet a left-handed person on a Tuesday morning. Any other day of the week, though, it is thought to be a good omen. This strange belief may stem from the fact that the Norse god Tiw was left-handed. Perhaps it was his left hand that was bitten off by the wolf Fenris. A more cheerful superstition is that couples who become engaged on a Tuesday will have a peaceful and contented life together.

Wednesday

Mercury's Day

The Babylonians believed the first hour of the fourth day was ruled over by the planet Mercury. The Romans called the fourth day *dies mercurii*, or Mercury's Day. Mercury was also the name of a Roman god. He wore a winged helmet, and was the messenger for all the other gods. In some countries, Wednesday is still named after the messenger god. In France the day is called Mercredi; in Spain, Miercoles; and in Italy, Mercoledi.

Other Christian and most non-Christian countries named the day after its position in the week — the Fourth Day, or Day Four. In Germany it is called Mittwoch, which means simply midweek.

Woden's Day

The Anglo-Saxons named the day after Woden, the chief of all their gods. They called it Woden's Tag. Woden was the god of wisdom, knowledge, and poetry. In the Norse legends Woden formed the earth from the body of a massive giant, Ymir. He fashioned humans from oak and elm trees. Woden was the wisest of all the gods. According to the legends he gave up one of his eyes for a drink from Mimir's well of knowledge. He saw everything and always knew exactly what all people were doing. In the great hall of Valhalla, Woden gathered his chosen warriors as they fell on the field of battle. In Asgard he rode an eight-footed horse, but often he traveled down to earth in disguise to mingle with ordinary mortals. He was a powerful magician, a sorcerer, and a healer. Sailors called on him to give them a fair wind. When the early Christians began converting the Saxons to their faith, they named Woden as the Devil.

By the time of the Crusades in the twelfth and thirteenth centuries, the name for the day had become Wodnesdai or Wodnesdawes. Shakespeare might have called it Weddensday or Wodynsday, while the Pilgrim Fathers might have said Weddinsday. The name became the one we know today about 250 years ago.

Solemn Wednesday

On Ash Wednesday Lent begins, and Christians all over the world begin their forty-day fast. The most devout Christians give up meat, eggs, and fats, but other people

give up only little treats, like biscuits or sweets. The day is called Ash Wednesday because, in the past, people going to church on this day would have ashes sprinkled over their heads. This custom was started by Gregory the Great, who was the Roman Catholic Pope 1,300 years ago. The custom remains in some Roman Catholic churches, where members of the congregation have crosses of ashes marked on their foreheads. Sometimes the ashes used are the remains of the palms scattered on Palm Sunday of the year before.

In the United States, in Maryland, ashes are scattered around fruit trees on Ash Wednesday. It is believed this will safeguard the trees from attack by pests all through the season.

In many countries the Wednesday before Easter is called Good Wednesday or Holy Wednesday, but in Ireland it is called Spy Wednesday. It is thought to be the day when Judas Iscariot bargained to become a spy against Jesus.

Thunder on a Wednesday is supposed to signify bloodshed, and in European tradition Wednesday is thought to be a very unlucky day. Americans, however, think that

the opposite is true, as this rhyme from New England shows:

> Monday for health,
> Tuesday for wealth,
> Wednesday the best of all.
> Thursday for losses,
> Friday for crosses,
> And Saturday no luck at all.

The birth of the sun and the moon

Persians regarded Wednesday as a very special day, because it was the day the sun and the moon were created. Indeed, it is the day on which all calendars began. In the Old Testament God is reported to have created the world in seven days. On the fourth day, Wednesday, He said: "Let there be lights in the firmament of the heaven to divide the day from the night; and let them be for signs, and for seasons, and for days, and years . . . and God made two great lights; the greater light to rule the day, and the lesser light to rule the night."

The greater light which ruled the day is, of course, the sun. The lesser light which ruled the night is the moon.

31

Thursday

Jupiter's Day

Thursday is the fifth day of the week. Its first hour, the Babylonians believed, was ruled by Jupiter. The Romans named the day after Jupiter, calling it *dies jovis*. The French, Spanish, and Italian names for the day are all based on the Roman one. In French it is called Jeudi; in Italian, Giovedi; and in Spanish, Jueves.

Jupiter was the ruler of all Roman gods, and he was also the god of thunder. Whenever he was painted or sculpted, he was shown as a man seated on a throne, holding a scepter in his left hand (a sign of kingship) and thunderbolts in his right hand.

Thor's Day

When the Anglo-Saxons came to name the day, they too chose a very powerful god — Thor. According to some legends he was the son of Woden, but other stories say that he was older and more powerful. Thor was the god of thunder who brought rain for the crops. His fame spread far and wide, and even the Normans worshipped him. They called him Thur, and made sacrifices to him before long sea voyages to bring them good weather.

Thor possessed a wonderful hammer called Miolner. Thunder was caused by Thor beating his hammer against his anvil. When he threw his hammer, it always returned to his hand like a boomerang. He wore an iron glove so that he could handle the hammer even when it was red hot. Thor had a magic belt which doubled his strength when he wore it, and he drove across the sky in a brass chariot drawn by two she-goats.

Days of thunder

Both the Roman Jupiter and the Saxon Thor were gods of thunder, and there has been a link between thunder and Thursday ever since ancient times. Thursday has often been called Thunderday. The Twelfth Legion of the ancient Roman army was called The Thundering Legion because they once prayed for rain during a terrible drought and were rewarded with a thunderstorm. The Legion carried an image of Jupiter on its flag.

The Anglo-Saxons called the day Thor's Tag. King Harold of England in 1066 would have called it Thorisdai, Thoresday, or Thorisday. King Henry VIII, nearly 500 years later, would have called it Thurisday. By the time Captain Cook was making his voyages to the South Seas towards the end of the eighteenth century the name had become Thursday.

In Germany Thor was called Donar, and their modern name for the day is Donnerstag. The Germans believe Thursday to be the unluckiest day of the week. Children should not be sent to school for the first time on a Thurs-

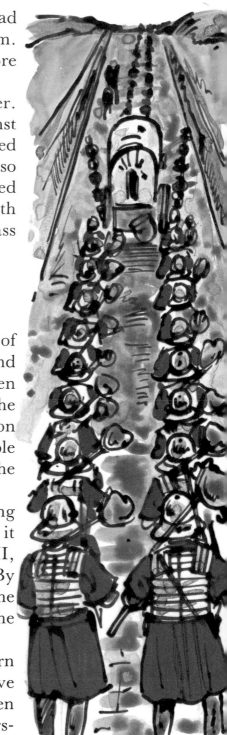

day nor should marriages be performed, nor any important business be undertaken.

Have you ever heard the expression, "When three Thursdays come together"? It means never, which makes sense when you think about it.

Black Thursday is very well known to Australians. On February 6, 1851, which was a Thursday, there was a terrible bush fire in the state of Victoria which killed many people.

There is a Swahili expression used by people in East Africa which says, "Every day is not Friday, there is also Thursday." Many people who speak Swahili are Moslems. Since Friday is a holy day to Moslems (see page 37), perhaps this is said to very religious people to remind them that there are other days of the week as well as the holy day, and that perhaps they should enjoy themselves a little more.

Maundy Thursday

One of the most important Thursdays in the Christian year is Maundy Thursday. Maundy Thursday, the fifth day of Holy Week, is the day before Good Friday. It is also called Great Thursday by members of the Greek Orthodox Church. On this Thursday Christ washed the feet of his disciples at the Last Supper, on the evening before his crucifixion. Later the custom arose for the feet of the poor to be washed by noblemen, priests, and even by the Pope and by Catholic kings and queens. This ceremony is still carried out in many Catholic cathedrals and monasteries.

In medieval times the washing ceremony was accompanied by gifts to poor people, in baskets called "maunds." This part of the ceremony survives in Britain

to this day. On Maundy Thursday every year, the king or queen of Great Britain gives gifts of ''Maundy money'' to aged, poor men and women — to as many people as there are years in the monarch's age. Each person receives one Maundy penny for each year of the reign.

Ascension Day

Forty days after Easter Christians celebrate Holy Thursday, or Ascension Day. This day commemorates the ascent of Jesus into heaven. It is believed that the weather should always be fine on Ascension Day because it is the day that Christ ''kissed the clouds.''

In old England, Holy Thursday was also called Bounds Thursday. Children, accompanied by clergymen and parish officers, would be walked around the parish boundaries on Bounds Thursday. Each boundary they would strike with a stick of willow. Sometimes the boys would be ''whipped'' or drenched with water to help them to remember where the boundaries were!

In Scotland the same ceremony was called ''riding the marches.'' A march is a boundary.

35

Friday

Venus's Day

Friday is the sixth day of the week. Babylonians believed its first hour was ruled over by the planet Venus. Venus was also the Roman's goddess of love, and they called Friday *dies veneris,* or Venus's Day. This is where the French, Italians, and Spanish get their modern names for the day. In France it is called Vendredi; in Italy, Venerdi; and in Spain, Viernes. In Welsh and in Hindu, too, the day is named after Venus.

Frigga's Day

The Anglo-Saxons named the day after their own goddess of married love, who was also the goddess of housewives, the sky, and the clouds. She was Frigga, the beautiful wife of the chief of the gods, Woden. Together they had seven sons who are supposed to have founded the seven Saxon kingdoms of England — Northumbria, Mercia, Wessex, East Anglia, Essex, Kent, and Sussex. Although Frigga was allowed to share the throne with Woden, she spent most of her time spinning and weaving, looking after the mortals who lived on earth and smoothing the paths of lovers and married people. She was also responsible for spreading knowledge and administering justice.

The Saxons called the sixth day of the week Frigga's Tag, and this is where the Germans get their modern name of the day from. They call it Freitag. Richard the Lionheart, who was king of England from 1189 to 1199, might have spelled it Fridaei, while Henry VIII would have written Frydaye. It became Friday around the time of the death of Queen Elizabeth I, at the beginning of the seventeenth century.

The Moslem Holy Day

Friday is a very important day for Moslems, many of whom live in the Arab countries of the Middle East, Iran, Afghanistan, Pakistan, and North Africa. It is the holiest day of their week, and is as important to them as Sunday is to Christians. The Moslems follow the teachings of the prophet Mohammed, who founded their religion 1,367 years ago. Friday is holy to them because it was on this day, in July 622, that Mohammed left the Arabian city of Mecca to go and preach in the desert. Arabs, and the Moslems of Pakistan, call the day al-Jumah, which

means "the day of the general assembly." Although Moslems have to say prayers five times every day, on Fridays they must gather to say the midday prayers in a mosque where a sermon may be preached from the pulpit.

As well as going to the mosque, some Moslems fast on this day. Cleansing of the body is another part of the Friday ritual.

Good Friday

One Friday of the year is a very holy day for Christians too. It is Good Friday, the Friday before Easter, the day on which Christ was crucified. It is called Good Friday because Jesus died for the good of mankind. Good Friday is celebrated by fasting, mourning, and other ceremonies by church-going people. A happy tradition on Good Friday is eating hot cross buns. They are marked with a cross because Christ was executed on a cross. The buns are warmed in the oven before eating. They used to be sold by street criers who would walk through the towns singing:

One a penny buns,
Two a penny buns,
If you have no daughters,
Give them to your sons.
One a penny,
Two a penny,
Hot cross buns.

Hot cross buns are eaten in Christian countries all over the world. In parts of Canada, though, a special loaf is baked on Good Friday. Some people used to believe that bread or buns baked on Good Friday would never get

38

moldy and would provide miraculous cures for all sorts of illnesses.

An unlucky day

Because it was the day on which Jesus was crucified, Friday is reckoned to be an unlucky day. It is also believed to be the day that Adam and Eve were expelled from the Garden of Eden, so it is doubly unlucky. American businessmen avoid starting new ventures on a Friday, while Scottish and English fishermen do not like to go to sea on this day. A Friday face, or Friday look, is used to describe anyone with a gloomy expression, while the French have this saying:

He who laughs on Friday will weep on Sunday.

If a Friday falls on the thirteenth day of the month it is especially unlucky. Thirteen is an unlucky number because there were thirteen people present at the Last Supper on the eve of Christ's death. Many people today are rather nervous on Friday the 13th.

However, Friday was a very lucky day for Mr. Crusoe. *Robinson Crusoe* is a famous story about a man who was shipwrecked on a Pacific island. Friday was the day he saw another human being after years of loneliness, and saved him from death. The man later became his servant, and Crusoe called him Man Friday. Today the term Man Friday or Girl Friday is used to describe someone who does all kinds of odd jobs in an office.

The weather on Friday is believed by some people to affect the weather on Sunday, as this French rhyme suggests:

Fine on Friday; fine on Sunday.
Wet on Friday; wet on Sunday.

39

Saturday

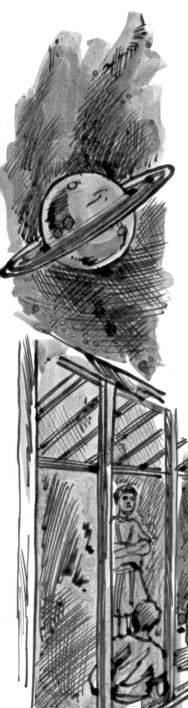

Saturn's Day

In Babylon, the planet that ruled the first hour of the sixth day was Saturn. Hundreds of years later the Romans had a god with the same name as the planet. He was Saturnus, the god of sowing or seed. Saturnus was a very ancient god, the father of Jupiter, Pluto, Neptune, and Juno, and the king of all the gods until dethroned by Jupiter. The remains of a temple built in honor of Saturn still stand in Rome today.

The Romans held a great festival for Saturnus in December. It was called Saturnalia, and was one of the most popular of all the Roman celebrations. It marked the beginning of the winter solstice (midwinter), a time when the Romans prayed to Saturnus to protect their winter-sown crops. During Saturnalia all work and busi-

40

ness ceased for seven days, slaves could be freed, no punishments could be handed out by the courts, and it was a time of merrymaking. A mock king, Saturn, was elected, and presents were exchanged.

Our modern festivals of Christmas and New Year both had their birth in this old Roman winter festival. Nobody knew exactly when Christ was born so during the fourth century the Church decided it should be celebrated during the winter solstice.

When the Romans named Saturday after Saturn they called it *dies saturni,* or Saturn's Day. The name for the day in many of the countries in Europe today is the same or similar. In Spain the day is called Saturno, and in Wales Dydd Sadwyn. England's Harold II in 1066 would have called it Seterdai or Zeterday. By the time William Caxton was printing the first book in English, 400 years later, it was called Saturnesday or Satirday. Someone living in 1604 might have called it Saturnsday. It was first called Saturday around the time of George Washington and Captain Cook in the 1770s.

In the Indian and Pakistani languages of Hindi and

ZETERDAY

SATURNSDAY

41

Urdu the day is also named after the planet Saturn. In Hindi it is called Sanivara, and in Urdu Sanichar. Sani, the name for the god of Saturn, is believed to be the god of misfortune. He is often shown to be a black man dressed all in black. Saturday is thought to be a very unlucky day in India. In other countries Saturn is called the god of death. It is believed that if you leave a hospital on Saturday you will soon be brought back. Saturday is also thought to be an unlucky day on which to move to another house or change jobs.

In Ireland people believe that a rainbow on a Saturday foretells a week of bad weather. In Scotland, a person born on that day is believed to have the power to see ghosts.

The Jewish sabbath

For Jewish people Saturday is the most important day of the week. It is their Sabbath, or Shabbat as they call it. The Bible states that God created the world in six days and rested on the seventh. Like the Christians, the Jews believe the seventh day should be a day of complete rest, but they believe God's day of rest was Saturday, not Sunday, and they are more strict about it than Christians. In Israel, the Jewish state, sabbath meals are prepared on the previous day, and there is no public transportation.

Shabbat means "to rest" in Hebrew, but it may come from the older Babylonian word Shapattu. Shapattu was a festival which the Babylonians held at each full moon. Like Shabbat, Shapattu meant "to rest."

The Jewish Sabbath begins at sunset on Friday (Friday is often called Erev Shabbat, or Sabbath eve) and lasts until nightfall on Saturday. There is a special service in the synagogue on Friday, and once this is over the family celebrates the beginning of the Sabbath with a special

candlelit meal. The custom is for a stranger, a traveler, a poor man, or a student to be invited to this shabbes meal, as it is called. On the Sabbath morning there is another service in the synagogue when Jews are reminded of one of the great stories of the Bible — of how their leader Moses was handed ten commandments by God, for the Jews to keep forever.

Some special sabbaths

Although every Sabbath is an important and holy day for Jews, there are a number of special Sabbaths. Shabbat Shuvah (Sabbath of Repentance) is the Sabbath between the Jewish festivals of Rosh Hashanah and Yom Kippur, and usually falls some time in October. On this Sabbath, special services of repentance are held in the synagogues. Shabbat Shirah (Sabbath of Song) does not occur on any particular date, but a special service is held in the synagogue which includes the reading of the Song of Moses and the Children of Israel in the Bible.

There are four special Sabbaths in spring — Shabbat Shekalin, Shabbat Zakhor (Sabbath of Remembrance), Shabbat Parah (Sabbath of the Red Heifer), and Shabbat ha-Hadesh. Shabbat Hazon (Sabbath of Vision) is the

43

sabbath before the ninth day of the Jewish month of Av. Usually this falls around July or August.

Christian Sundays

Although in Christian countries the day of rest is Sunday, the Greeks, Italians, and Portuguese all call Saturday the Sabbath. In Greek it is called Sabbaton, in Italian it is Sabato, and in Portuguese it is Sabado.

Christians do have some special Saturdays in the year, however. The Saturday before Lent used to be called Egg Saturday in some parts of Britain, probably because it was the time when all the eggs in the house were eaten up before the Lenten fast. The Saturday between Good Friday and Easter Sunday is important too, and in some Christian countries it is called Holy Saturday.

Because Saturday was the eve of their day of rest, it was welcomed heartily by the slaves of the American cotton plantations, and they had this saying:

Saturday night help the rheumatism powerful.

It was probably the only night of the week when they could look forward to sleep without having to worry about working hard the next day.

44

The days around the world

Days named after gods

Several countries of northern Europe have names for the days of the week very similar to the English names. This is because these are the countries that were colonized by the Romans and the Saxons, and many words of their languages continue to be used today. The names for the days of the week are based on the names of Roman and Saxon gods.

Days named after planets

Other European countries use only the Roman names for the "planets" — sun, moon, Mars, Mercury, Jupiter, Venus, and Saturn. These countries were never overrun by the Saxons, and therefore never spoke their language or became interested in their gods. The Hindus of India, who speak Hindi, and the Moslems of Pakistan, who speak Urdu, use names for the days based on their own names for the planets. However, because Pakistan is a Moslem country, the holy day of Friday is called by the Arabic name Jumah, which means the day of the assembly; and the name of Thursday, Jumarat, means the day before Jumah.

Numbered days

A few European countries, and many countries outside Europe, give numbers to the days instead of names. In

English	Sunday	Monday	Tuesday
German	Sonntag	Montag	Dienstag
Dutch and Flemish	Zondag	Maandag	Dinsdag
Swedish	Sondag	Mandag	Tisdag
Danish	Søndag	Mandag	Tirsdag
French	Dimanche	Lundi	Mardi
Spanish	Domingo	Lunes	Martes
Italian	Domenica	Lunedi	Martedi
Welsh	Dydd Sul	Dydd Llun	Dydd Mawrth
Hindi	Ravivara	Somavara	Mangalavara
Urdu	Itvar	Pirvar	Mangalvar
Hebrew	Yom Rison	Yom Sheni	Yom Shlishi
Arabic	Yawm al-Ahad	Yawm al-Ithnayn	Yawm al-Thalatha
Portuguese	Domingo	Segunda-feira	Terca-feira
Greek	Kiriaki	Theftera	Triti
Chinese	Xing-qi tian	Xing-qi yi	Xing-qi er
Swahili	Jumapili	Jumatatu	Jumanne

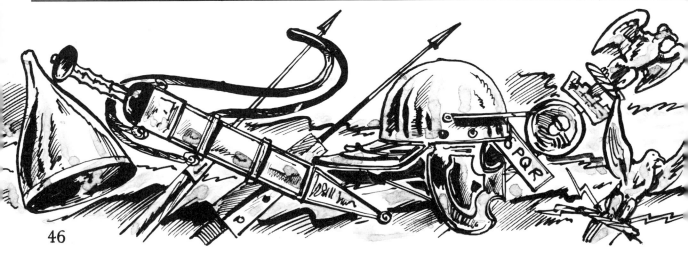

Wednesday	Thursday	Friday	Saturday
Mittwoch	Donnerstag	Freitag	Samstag
Woensdag	Donderdag	Vrijdag	Zaterdag
Onsdag	Torsdag	Fredag	Lordag
Onsdag	Torsdag	Fredag	Lørdag
Mercredi	Jeudi	Vendredi	Samedi
Miercoles	Jueves	Viernes	Sabado
Mercoledi	Giovedi	Venerdi	Sabato
Dydd Mercher	Dydd Iau	Dydd Gwener	Dydd Sadwrn
Budhavara	Brhaspativara	Sukravara	Sanivara
Budhvar	Jumarat	Jumah	Sanichar
Yom Revie	Yom Hamishi	Yom Shishi	Yom Shabbat
Yawm al-Arbaa	Yawm al-Khamis	Al-Jumah	Al-Sabt
Quarta-feira	Quinta-feira	Sexta-feira	Sabado
Tetarti	Pempti	Paraskeri	Sabbaton
Xing-qi san	Xing-qi si	Xing-qi wu	Xing-qi liu
Jumatano	Alhamisi	Ijumaa	Jumamosi

the Christian European countries the days are usually numbered from Sunday to Saturday. However, Sunday is not actually called Day One but the Lord's Day. Arabic and Hebrew speakers do call Sunday Day One, as it is not a holy day to them. In China the days are numbered from Monday to Sunday.

In Swahili, the language widely spoken in East Africa, the days are numbered from Friday to Thursday because many of the people are Moslem, and Friday is the Moslem holy day. However, the first day is not called Day One but Ijumaa — the day of the general assembly. The word for Saturday means Ijumaa Plus One, Sunday is Ijumaa Plus Two, and so on.

However, Thursday is actually called Day Five instead of Ijumaa Plus Six. This is because they have kept the old name for Thursday, from before the country was Moslem. The old week used to be numbered from Sunday so naturally Thursday was Day Five. It must be

rather confusing nowadays, however, with Ijumaa Plus Five followed by Day Five!

Names of the days in other languages

The table on pages 46 and 47 lists seventeen languages but it covers over 100 countries. Between the sixteenth and twentieth centuries, the Spanish, Portuguese, British, French, and other empires spread their languages all over the world.

English is used as the official language, or a very common language, in Australia, Belize, Botswana, Canada, Eire, Fiji, Ghana, Guyana, Hong Kong, India, Jamaica, Kenya, Malawi, Malaysia, New Zealand, Nigeria, Pakistan, Papua-New Guinea, Philippines, Singapore, South Africa, Sri Lanka, Swaziland, Tanzania, Uganda, the United States, Zambia, and other countries.

French is used similarly in Algeria, Belgium, Benin, Canada, Chad, Congo, Luxembourg, Mali, Niger, Switzerland, Syria, Zaire, and other countries.

Spanish is used similarly in Argentina, Bolivia, Chile, Columbia, Costa Rica, Cuba, Dominican Republic, Ecuador, Guatemala, Honduras, Mexico, Nicaragua, Panama, Peru, Puerto Rico, Venezuela, and other countries.

Portuguese is used similarly in Angola, Brazil, Mozambique, and other countries.

German is used similarly in Austria and Switzerland.

Dutch is the basis of the Afrikaans language used in South Africa.

Arabic is used in Arabia, Egypt, Sudan, Lebanon, Syria, Iraq, Israel, Algeria, Morocco, and other countries.

Swahili is used in Kenya, Uganda, Tanzania, Zaire, and other countries.

49

The perpetual calendar

Have you ever wondered what day of the week the Battle of Concord was fought on, or the American Declaration of Independence was issued, or Captain Cook first sighted Australia, or the Boers began their Great Trek?

You can find out with the perpetual calendar. In fact you can use it to discover the day of the week for any date in history between the year 0 and 2399.

The perpetual calendar looks complicated at first, but it is really very easy. Here is an example. Let us discover on which day of the week William Shakespeare was born. His birthday is believed to be April 23, 1564.

Seven simple stages bring you to the answer.

First Table

1. In the table on pages 54 and 55, the columns numbered 1-12 are for the centuries. Column 2 shows the three centuries 100-199, 800-899, and 1500-1599. As Shakespeare was born between 1500 and 1599, that is the column we want.

2. Down the left side are four rows of numbers — one number for each year of the century. As Shakespeare was born in the 64th year, look for the number 64. It is in the eighth row down.

3. Look along that row until you reach Column 2. There you will see a letter code — BA.

4. Most codes have only one letter. The ones with two letters are for leap years. If the date is in January or February, use the first letter. If it is in any other month, use the second letter. As Shakespeare's birthday was in April, we use the second letter — A.

51

Now that you have the code letter, transfer to the second table on pages 56 and 57.

Second Table

5. In this table, find the month of April on the left-hand side, then look along the row of letters until you find your code letter A. It is in Column 2.

6. Now move down to the section marked Days. As Shakespeare was born on the 23rd day, look for the number 23. It is in the second row.

7. Look along the row until you reach Column 2, where the code letter A is, and there you will find which day of the week Shakespeare was born. It was a Sunday.

Once you have learned to use the perpetual calendar it takes only a few seconds to look up any date. Here are a few more days to find (the answers are on page 59).

1. Battle of Trafalgar and death of Nelson (October 21, 1805)
2. Beginning of the First World War (August 4, 1914)
3. Japanese attack on Pearl Harbor (December 7, 1941)
4. Conquest of Mt. Everest by Edmund Hillary of New Zealand and Tensing Norgay of Nepal (May 29, 1953)
5. First men on the moon (July 21, 1969)

The Julian and Gregorian calendars

In the first table you will see there is a slight gap between Columns 7 and 8. That is to show where the calendar first changed from the Julian calendar to the Gregorian calendar. The Julian calendar was drawn up by Julius Caesar about 2,000 years ago. But it was slightly inaccurate, so in 1582 Pope Gregory announced a new calendar that was more accurate.

All dates of the Julian calendar are in Columns 1 to 7.

For dates after October 4, 1582, you must be careful. Countries changed from the Julian to the Gregorian calendar at different times. You need to know if the date is Julian or Gregorian. Sometimes this information is very difficult to discover, but your librarian can probably help you.

Britain and its colonies did not change to the Gregorian calendar until 1752. Most history books in the English language use the Julian calendar for dates up to September 3, 1752, but it is always worth checking to be sure that the date is not a Gregorian one if it falls between 1582 and 1752.

				1	2	3	4	5
				0	100	200	300	400
				700	800	900	1000	1100
				1400	1500	1600	1700	
0				—	ED	FE	GF	AG
1	29	57	85	B	C	D	E	F
2	30	58	86	A	B	C	D	E
3	31	59	87	G	A	B	C	D
4	32	60	88	FE	GF	AG	BA	CB
5	33	61	89	D	E	F	G	A
6	34	62	90	C	D	E	F	G
7	35	63	91	B	C	D	E	F
8	36	64	92	AG	BA	CB	DC	ED
9	37	65	93	F	G	A	B	C
10	38	66	94	E	F	G	A	B
11	39	67	95	D	E	F	G	A
12	40	68	96	CB	DC	ED	FE	GF
13	41	69	97	A	B	C	D	E
14	42	70	98	G	A	B	C	D
15	43	71	99	F	G	A	B	C
16	44	72		ED	FE	GF	AG	BA
17	45	73		C	D	E	F	G
18	46	74		B	C	D	E	F
19	47	75		A	B	C	D	E
20	48	76		GF	AG	BA	CB	DC
21	49	77		E	F	G	A	B
22	50	78		D	E	F	G	A
23	51	79		C	D	E	F	G
24	52	80		BA	CB	DC	ED	FE
25	53	81		G	A	B	C	D
26	54	82		F	G	A	B	C
27	55	83		E	F	G	A	B
28	56	84		DC	ED	FE	GF	AG

6	7	8	9	10	11	12
500	600	1500	1600	1700	1800	1900
1200	1300		2000	2100	2200	2300
BA	CB	—	BA	C	E	G
G	A	F	G	B	D	F
F	G	E	F	A	C	E
E	F	D	E	G	B	D
DC	ED	CB	DC	FE	AG	CB
B	C	A	B	D	F	A
A	B	G	A	C	E	G
G	A	F	G	B	D	F
FE	GF	ED	FE	AG	CB	ED
D	E	C	D	F	A	C
C	D	B	C	E	G	B
B	C	A	B	D	F	A
AG	BA	GF	AG	CB	ED	GF
F	G	E	F	A	C	E
E	F	D	E	G	B	D
D	E	C	D	F	A	C
CB	DC	—	CB	ED	GF	BA
A	B	—	A	C	E	G
G	A	—	G	B	D	F
F	G	—	F	A	C	E
ED	FE	—	ED	GF	BA	DC
C	D	—	C	E	G	B
B	C	—	B	D	F	A
A	B	—	A	C	E	G
GF	AG	—	GF	BA	DC	FE
E	F	—	E	G	B	D
D	E	C	D	F	A	C
C	D	B	C	E	G	B
BA	CB	AG	BA	DC	FE	AG

	1	2
January/October	A	B
February/March/November	D	E
April/July	G	A
May	B	C
June	E	F
August	C	D
September/December	F	G

Days

					1	2
1	8	15	22	29	Sunday	Saturday
2	9	16	23	30	Monday	Sunday
3	10	17	24	31	Tuesday	Monday
4	11	18	25		Wednesday	Tuesday
5	12	19	26		Thursday	Wednesday
6	13	20	27		Friday	Thursday
7	14	21	28		Saturday	Friday

3	4	5	6	7
C	D	E	F	G
F	G	A	B	C
B	C	D	E	F
D	E	F	G	A
G	A	B	C	D
E	F	G	A	B
A	B	C	D	E

Friday	Thursday	Wednesday	Tuesday	Monday
Saturday	Friday	Thursday	Wednesday	Tuesday
Sunday	Saturday	Friday	Thursday	Wednesday
Monday	Sunday	Saturday	Friday	Thursday
Tuesday	Monday	Sunday	Saturday	Friday
Wednesday	Tuesday	Monday	Sunday	Saturday
Thursday	Wednesday	Tuesday	Monday	Sunday

57

Glossary

Babylonians An ancient race of people who lived in the Euphrates Valley, now a part of Iraq.

calendar A system of measuring the passing of the years and parts of years.

Catholic A Christian who believes the Pope is God's representative on earth.

Christian A follower of the religion founded in the first century by Jesus Christ.

crucifixion Execution by being strung or nailed upon a cross-shaped gallows and left to die. This was the fate of Jesus Christ.

day The time taken by the earth to rotate once on its own axis.

Christmas The annual festival in December that commemorates the birth of Jesus Christ.

Easter An annual festival on a Sunday in March or April that celebrates the death and rebirth of Jesus Christ.

fasting Going without food, or eating very little, for religious reasons as a form of self-denial.

Good Friday The Friday before Easter that commemorates the crucifixion of Jesus Christ.

Jesus Christ The Jewish founder of the Christian religion. Christians believe He is the son of God and that three days after being crucified He came to life again to live in Heaven.

The calendar used in most countries dates from the year of His birth.

Jew A follower of the Jewish religion, descended from the Hebrews of Biblical times who lived in the country now called Israel.

Lent A period of forty days' fasting and penitence before Easter.

Mohammed The Arab founder of the Moslem religion who lived from approximately 570 to 632.

month The approximate time taken by the moon to make one orbit of the earth.

Moslem A follower of the Moslem religion founded by Mohammed in Arabia in the seventh century.

mosque A Moslem church.

New Testament A collection of sacred books telling the story of Jesus Christ's life and the spread of his teaching. Together with the Old Testament it forms the Christian holy book, the Bible.

Normans A race of people from Normandy in France who conquered and settled in England in the eleventh century.

Old Testament A collection of the sacred books of the Jews.

Orthodox Church The Christian Church of eastern Europe and western Asia which does not accept the authority of the Pope, who is head of the Catholic Church.

planets The heavenly bodies that

58

revolve around the sun — Mercury, Venus, Earth, Mars, Jupiter, Saturn, Uranus, Neptune, and Pluto. In ancient times Uranus, Neptune, and Pluto had not been discovered, but the sun and the moon were also regarded as planets.

Pope The head of the Catholic Church.

Romans The ancient race of people who had their capital at Rome and who established an empire covering much of Europe, northern Africa, and the Middle East.

sabbath A day of rest and worship, held by Moslems on Friday, Jews on Saturday, and Christians on Sunday.

Saxons A race of Germanic people who settled in England in the fifth and sixth centuries.

synagogue A Jewish church.

year The time taken by the earth to make one orbit of the sun. For the sake of the Gregorian calendar, this is regarded as 365 or 366 days.

Answers to questions on page 52:
1. Monday
2. Tuesday
3. Sunday
4. Friday
5. Monday

59

Index